MAN-MADE DISASTERS
DEEPWATER HORIZON

by Nikole Brooks Bethea

pogo

Ideas for Parents and Teachers

Pogo Books let children practice reading informational text while introducing them to nonfiction features such as headings, labels, sidebars, maps, and diagrams, as well as a table of contents, glossary, and index.

Carefully leveled text with a strong photo match offers early fluent readers the support they need to succeed.

Before Reading

- "Walk" through the book and point out the various nonfiction features. Ask the student what purpose each feature serves.

- Look at the glossary together. Read and discuss the words.

Read the Book

- Have the child read the book independently.

- Invite him or her to list questions that arise from reading.

After Reading

- Discuss the child's questions. Talk about how he or she might find answers to those questions.

- Prompt the child to think more. Ask: Did you know about the *Deepwater Horizon* disaster before reading this book? What more do you want to learn after reading it?

Pogo Books are published by Jump!
5357 Penn Avenue South
Minneapolis, MN 55419
www.jumplibrary.com

Library of Congress Cataloging-in-Publication Data

Names: Bethea, Nikole Brooks, author.
Title: Deepwater Horizon / by Nikole Brooks Bethea.
Description: Minneapolis, MN: Jump!, Inc., [2018]
Series: Man-made disasters | Audience: Ages 7-10.
Includes bibliographical references and index.
Identifiers: LCCN 2017027408 (print)
LCCN 2017027728 (ebook)
ISBN 9781624967030 (ebook)
ISBN 9781620319185 (hardcover: alk. paper)
ISBN 9781620319192 (pbk.)
Subjects: LCSH: BP Deepwater Horizon Explosion and Oil Spill, 2010–Juvenile literature. | Deepwater Horizon (Drilling rig)–Juvenile literature. | Oil wells–Mexico, Gulf of–Blowouts–History–21st century–Juvenile literature. | Oil spills–Mexico, Gulf of–History–21st century–Juvenile literature. | Oil spills–Environmental aspects–Mexico, Gulf of–History–21st century–Juvenile literature.
Classification: LCC TN871.215 (ebook) | LCC TN871.215. B48 2018 (print) | DDC 363.738/20916364–dc23
LC record available at https://lccn.loc.gov/2017027408

Editor: Kristine Spanier
Book Designer: Michelle Sonnek
Photo Researcher: Michelle Sonnek

Photo Credits: US Coast Guard/Getty Images, cover; landbysea/iStock, 1 (background), 4; BortN66/Shutterstock, 1 (foreground); mjaud/Shutterstock, 3; tomom pukesom/Shutterstock, 5; Jon T. Fritz/MCT, 6-7; Stocktrek Images, Inc./Alamy, 8; Xinhua/BP Live Feed/Photoshot, 9 (leak); Baloncici/Shutterstock, 9 (monitor); Louisiana Governors Office/Alamy, 10-11; NOAA/Alamy, 12-13; Africa Studio/Shutterstock, 14; Associated Press/AP Images, 15; Craig Ruttle/Alamy, 16-17, Oil and Gas Photographer/Shutterstock, 18-19; Steve Bower/Shutterstock, 20-21; rnl/Shutterstock, 23.

Printed in the United States of America at Corporate Graphics in North Mankato, Minnesota.

TABLE OF CONTENTS

CHAPTER 1

BLOWOUT

It was April 20, 2010. An **oil rig** floated in the Gulf of Mexico. Its name was *Deepwater Horizon*.

Its crew had drilled a well. It was 13,000 feet (3,962 meters) below the seafloor. It reached a supply of oil and gas. The oil collected would be used for **fuel**.

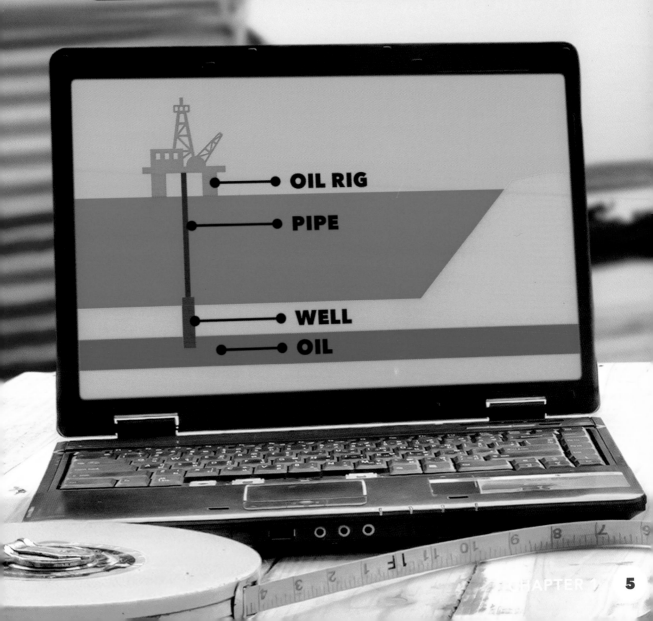

OIL RIG

PIPE

WELL

OIL

Boom! An explosion rocked the rig. Boom! There was another. The power went out. Fires blazed. Workers rushed to lifeboats. Some jumped into the water below.

What happened? There was a **blowout** in the well. Its design was flawed. Gas came up through the well. It flowed onto the rig. It **ignited**.

Eleven crew members died. Seventeen were hurt.

CHAPTER 2

OIL SPILL

The rig burned for two days. Then it sank. The pipe connecting the rig to the well broke. Oil spilled into the water.

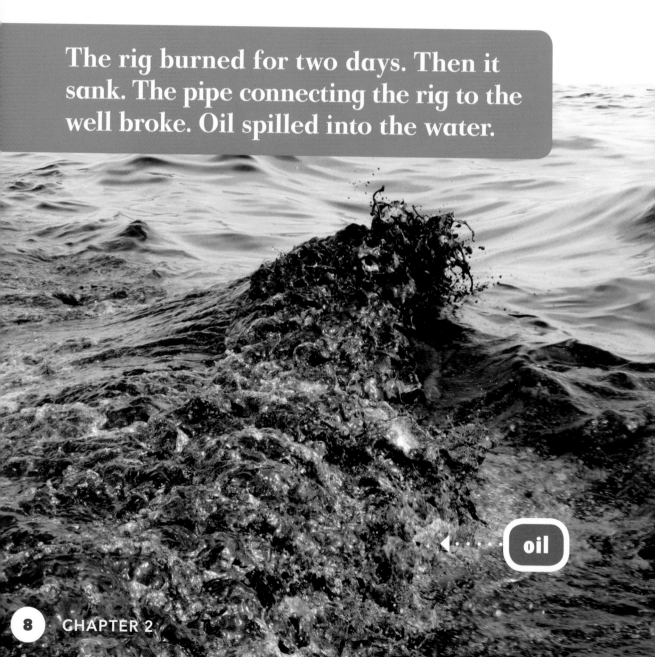

oil

Stopping the flow wasn't easy. It was almost one mile (1.6 kilometers) underwater.

They tried many things. A large dome was placed over the leak. It was meant to catch the oil. A pipe would send the oil up to a ship. But its opening clogged. It failed.

oil ·····▶

Workers tried placing trash into the well. This included golf balls and shredded tires. Mud was pumped in. But this failed, too. The oil pushed the trash and mud out.

Finally, underwater robots placed a cap on the well. The oil flow stopped on July 15, 2010. It had been 87 days. About five million barrels spilled. It was the largest oil spill in U.S. history.

DID YOU KNOW?

Oil comes from ancient plants and animals. They died. Their remains sank to the seafloor. They decayed. Sand covered them. Heat and **pressure** transformed them. They turned into **crude oil** and natural gas.

OIL

How did they try to clean the water? They added **dispersants**. These break down oil. This speeds up natural **biodegradation**. Tiny ocean **microbes** ate some of the oil. Boats **skimmed** floating oil off the surface.

Long floating barriers were placed along shores. They kept some of the oil from coming onshore.

skimming oil

TAKE A LOOK!

The oil spill grew. It covered an area the size of the state of Virginia.

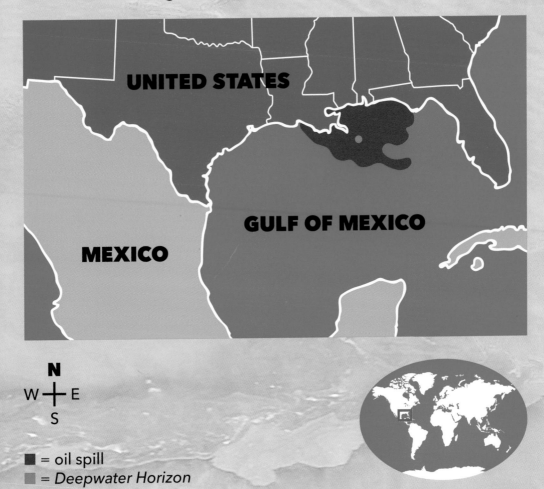

UNITED STATES

MEXICO

GULF OF MEXICO

N
W ┼ E
S

■ = oil spill
■ = *Deepwater Horizon*

CHAPTER 3

DAMAGE

Oil covered 43,300 square miles (112,146 square kilometers) of the gulf. Winds blew. Currents flowed. Tides rose and fell. Oil moved toward the coast. It reached 1,300 miles (2,092 km) of shoreline.

Beaches closed. People couldn't fish. **Habitats** such as marshes, wetlands, and coral were damaged.

Wildlife suffered. Birds, sea turtles, and marine animals were covered in oil. Thousands died. Shrimp, crab, and oyster populations were harmed.

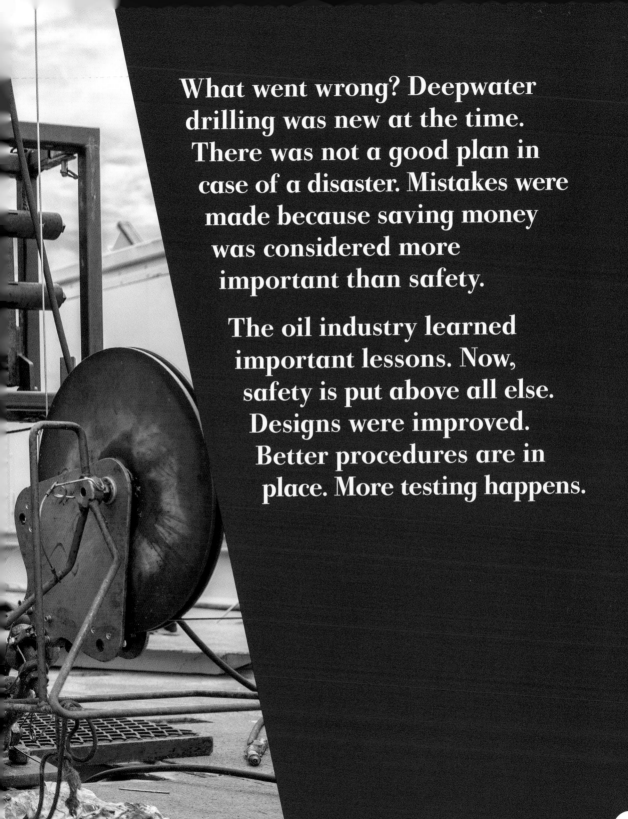

What went wrong? Deepwater drilling was new at the time. There was not a good plan in case of a disaster. Mistakes were made because saving money was considered more important than safety.

The oil industry learned important lessons. Now, safety is put above all else. Designs were improved. Better procedures are in place. More testing happens.

It may be years before all the damage is fully understood. But the Gulf Coast is slowly recovering.

ACTIVITIES & TOOLS

OIL SPILL ACTIVITY

**How hard is it to clean up oil?
What materials make it easier?
Find out in this activity.**

What You Need:
- shallow dish
- small bowl
- water
- 3 Tbsp. vegetable oil
- 2 Tbsp. cocoa powder
- cotton ball
- sponge
- paper towel

① **Fill dish ¾ full with water.**

② **In a bowl, mix vegetable oil and cocoa powder. This represents crude oil.**

③ **Slowly pour the oily mixture into the water. Wait three minutes. Does the mixture sink or float?**

④ **Place the cotton ball in the center of your oil slick. Does it remove the oil?**

⑤ **Repeat step 4 with the sponge and paper towel.**

⑥ **Can you think of other ways to get the oil out of the water?**

GLOSSARY

biodegradation: The breakdown of materials by bacteria or other organisms.

blowout: An uncontrolled flow of gas or oil from a reservoir to the surface.

crude oil: Oil from below Earth's surface that is used to make gasoline and other fuels.

dispersants: Chemicals that break down oil and speed up natural biodegradation.

fuel: A material, such as gasoline, that is burned to make heat or power.

habitats: The natural environments or homes of plants and animals.

ignited: Caught on fire.

microbes: Extremely small living things you can only see with a microscope.

oil rig: A structure above an oil well that contains equipment for removing oil from the ground.

pressure: The force or weight that is put on something.

skimmed: Used a device to remove oil floating on water.

INDEX

TO LEARN MORE

Learning more is as easy as 1, 2, 3.

1) Go to www.factsurfer.com
2) Enter "DeepwaterHorizon" into the search box.
3) Click the "Surf" button to see a list of websites.

With factsurfer, finding more information is just a click away.